This book belongs to

Thank you for giving color to this book

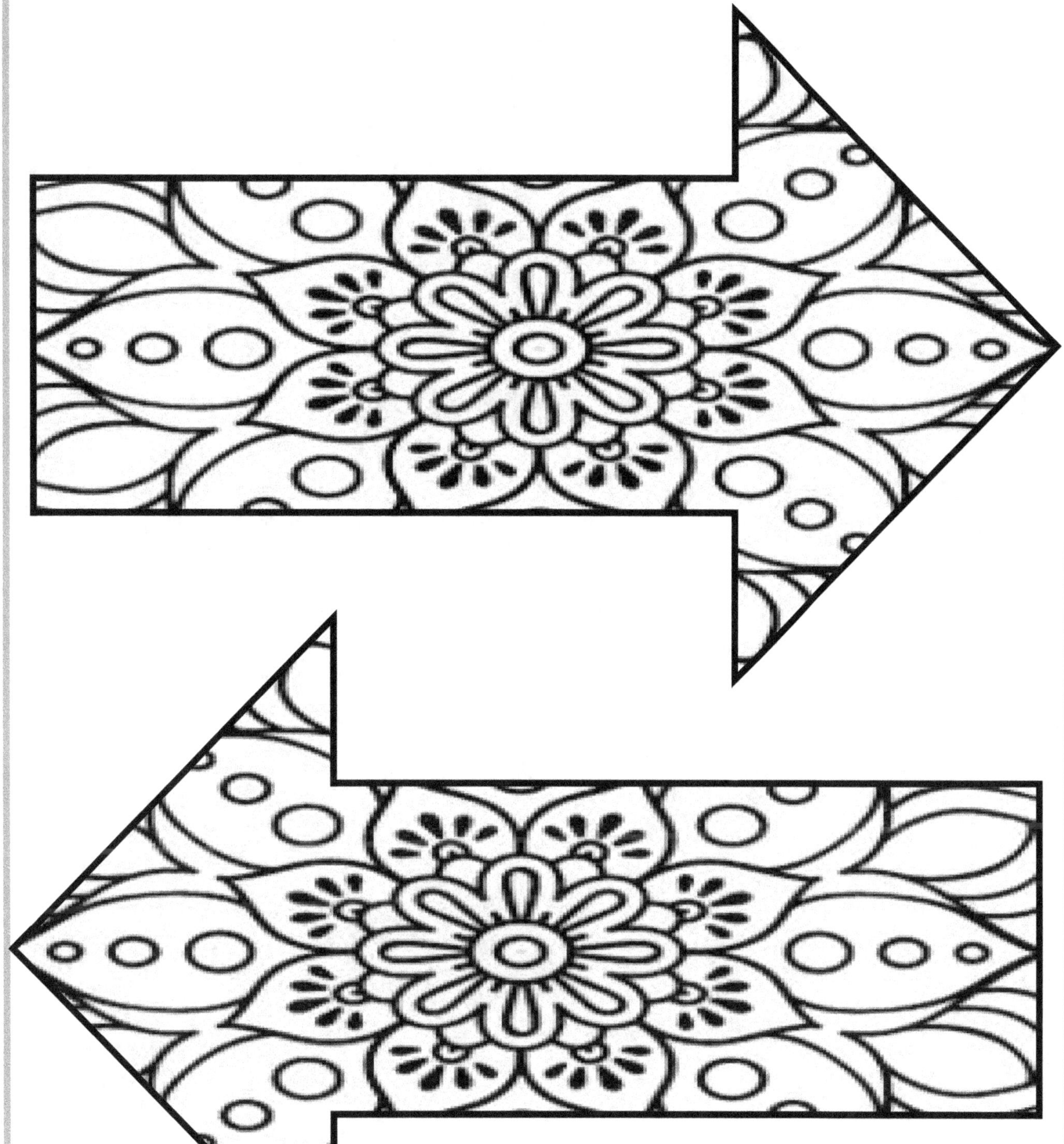

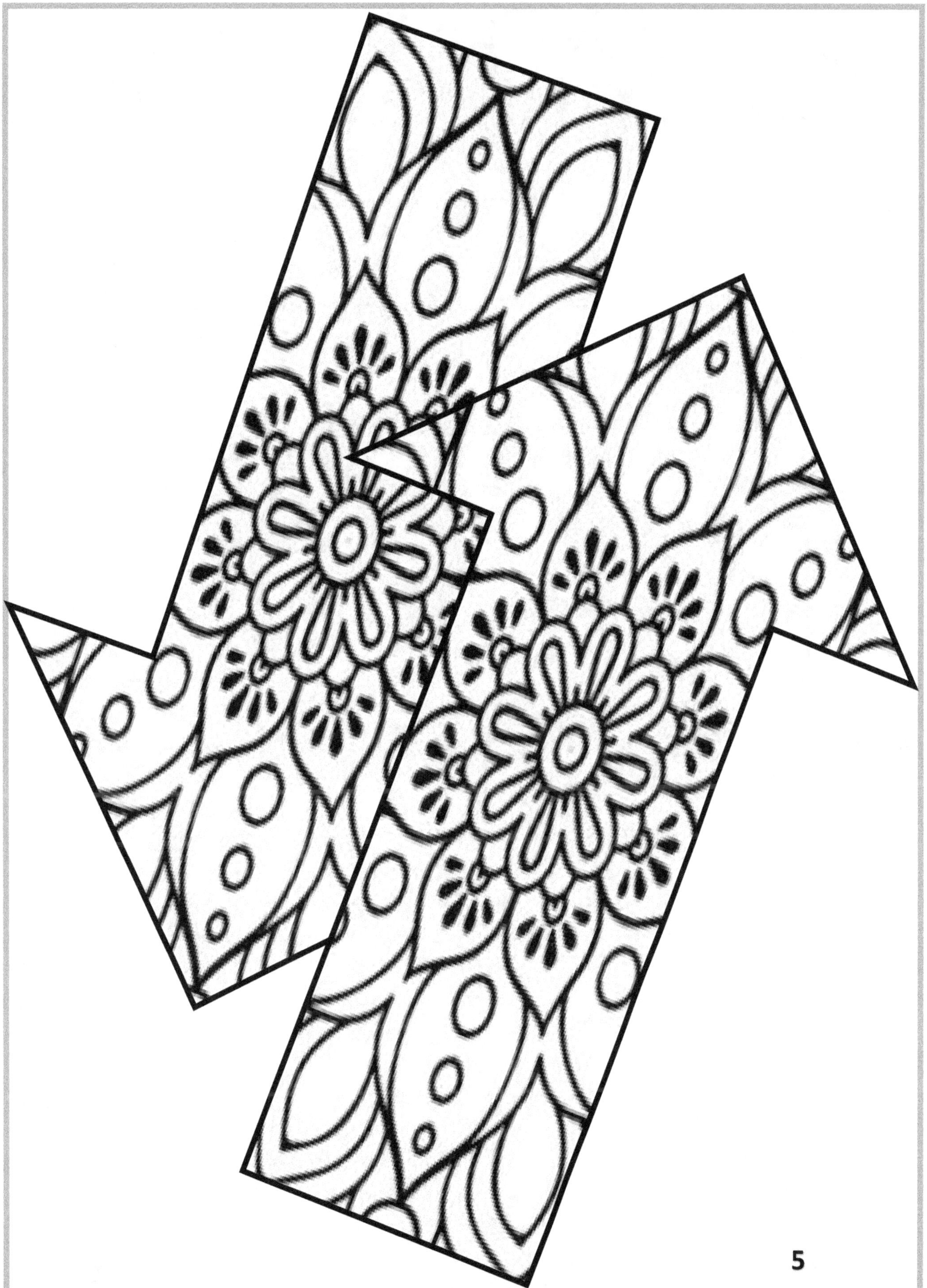

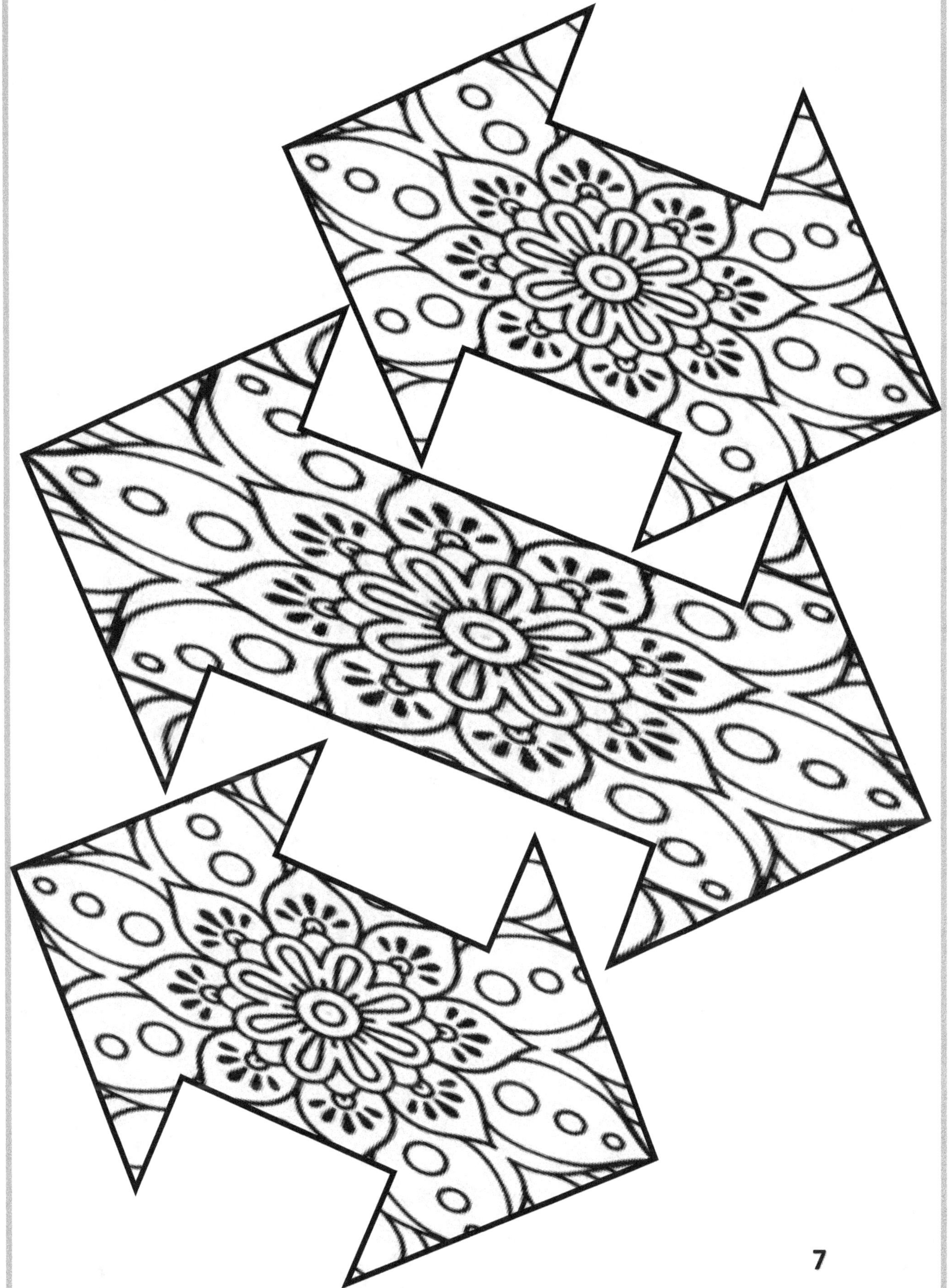

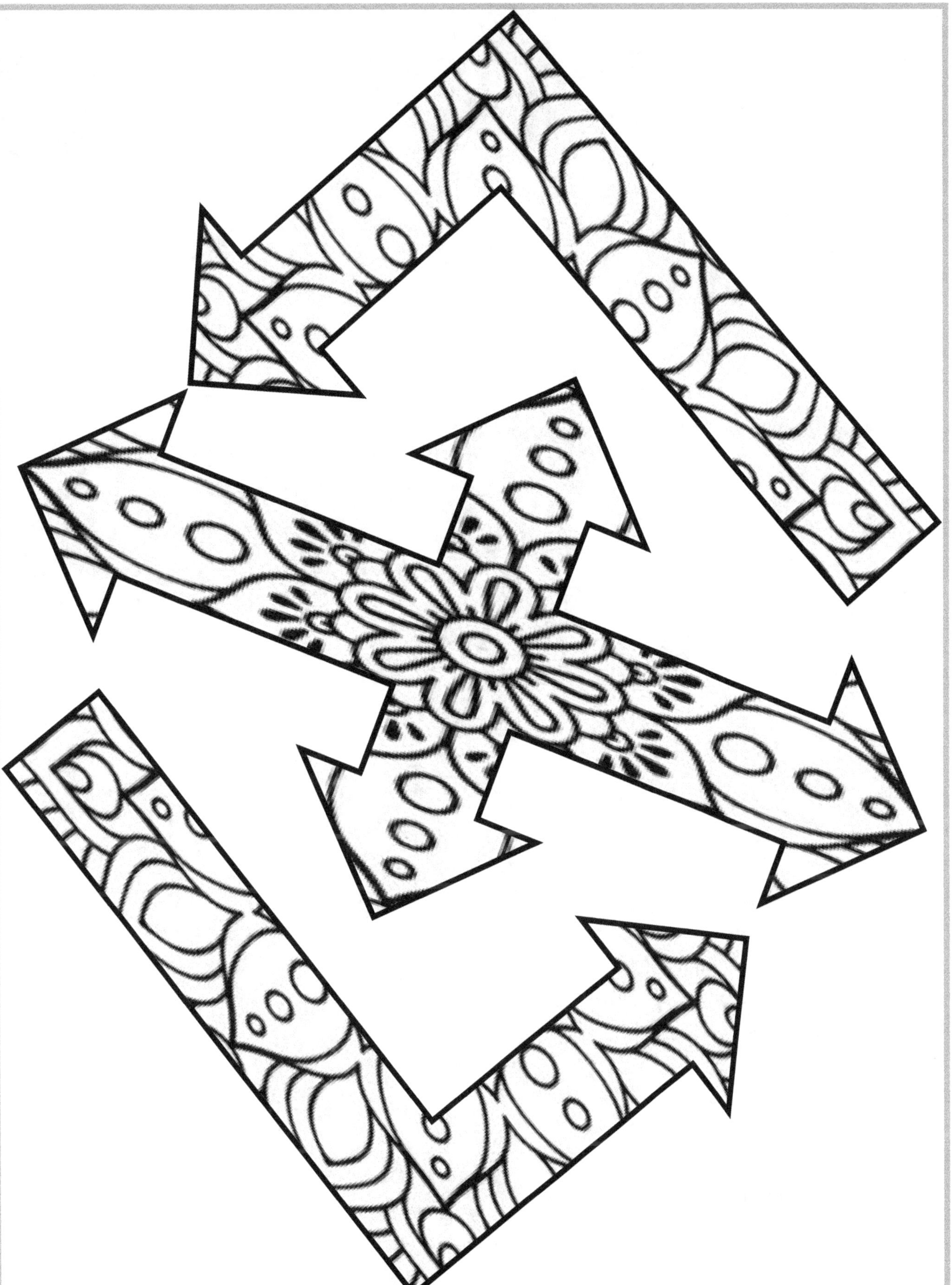

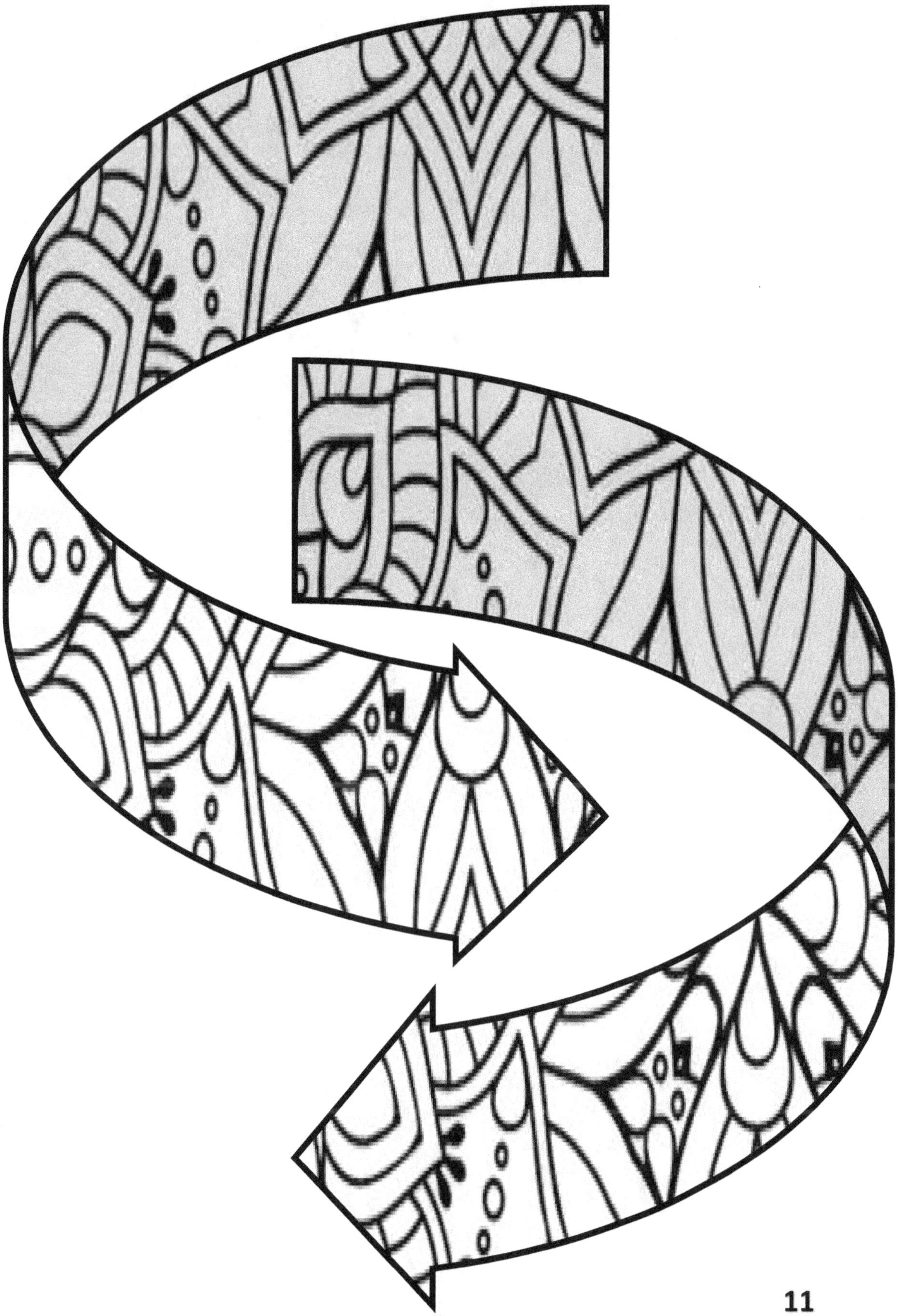

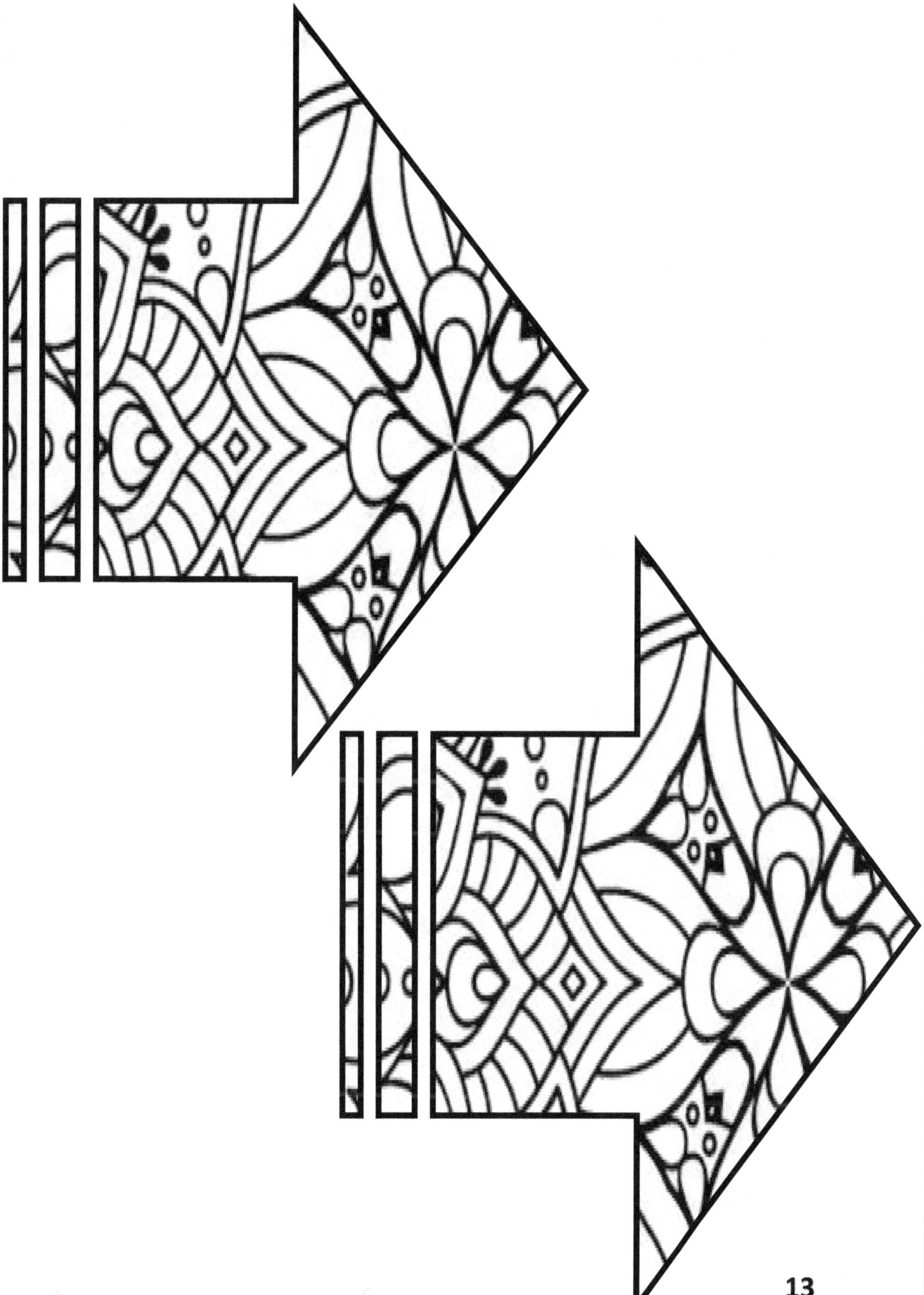

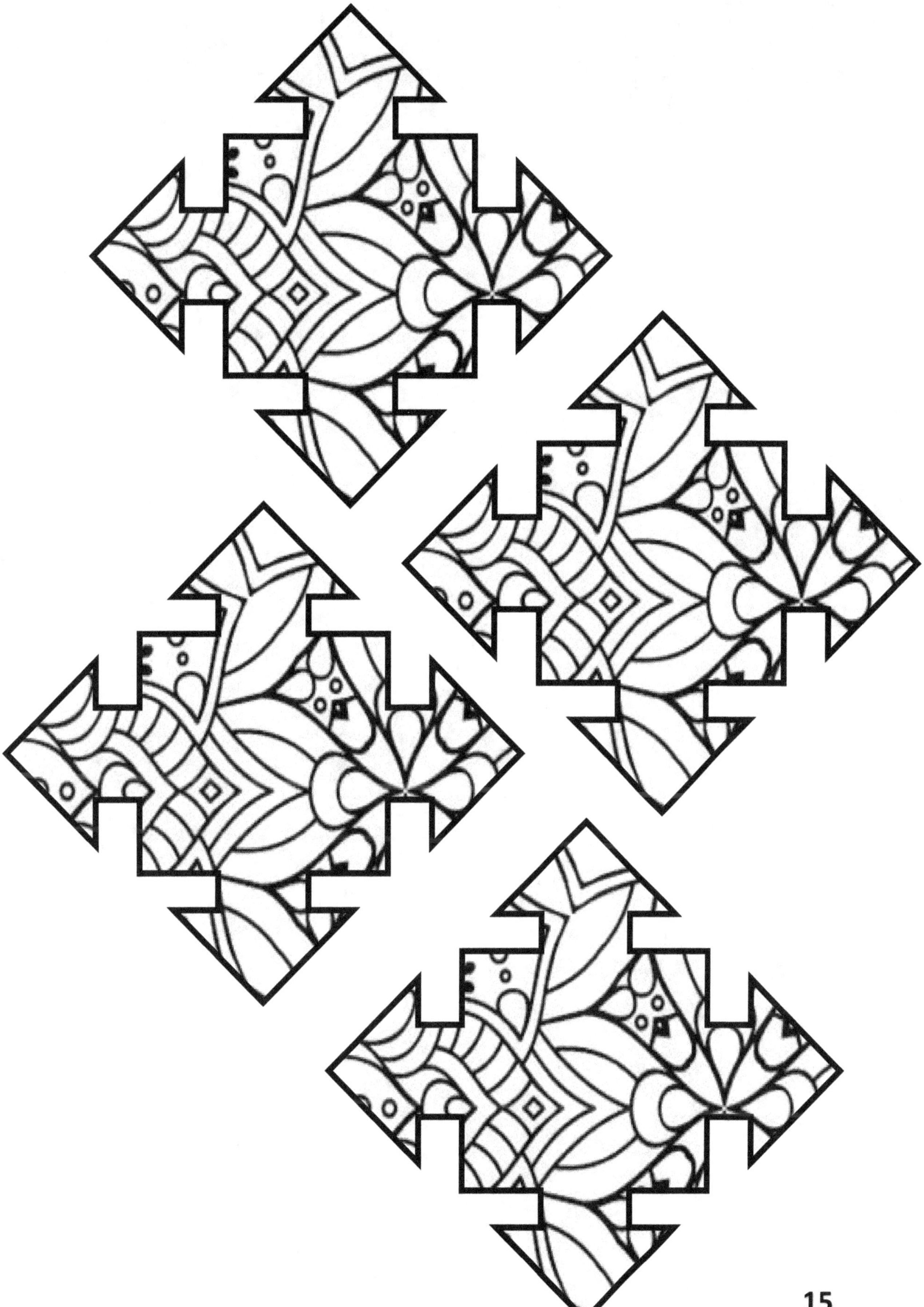

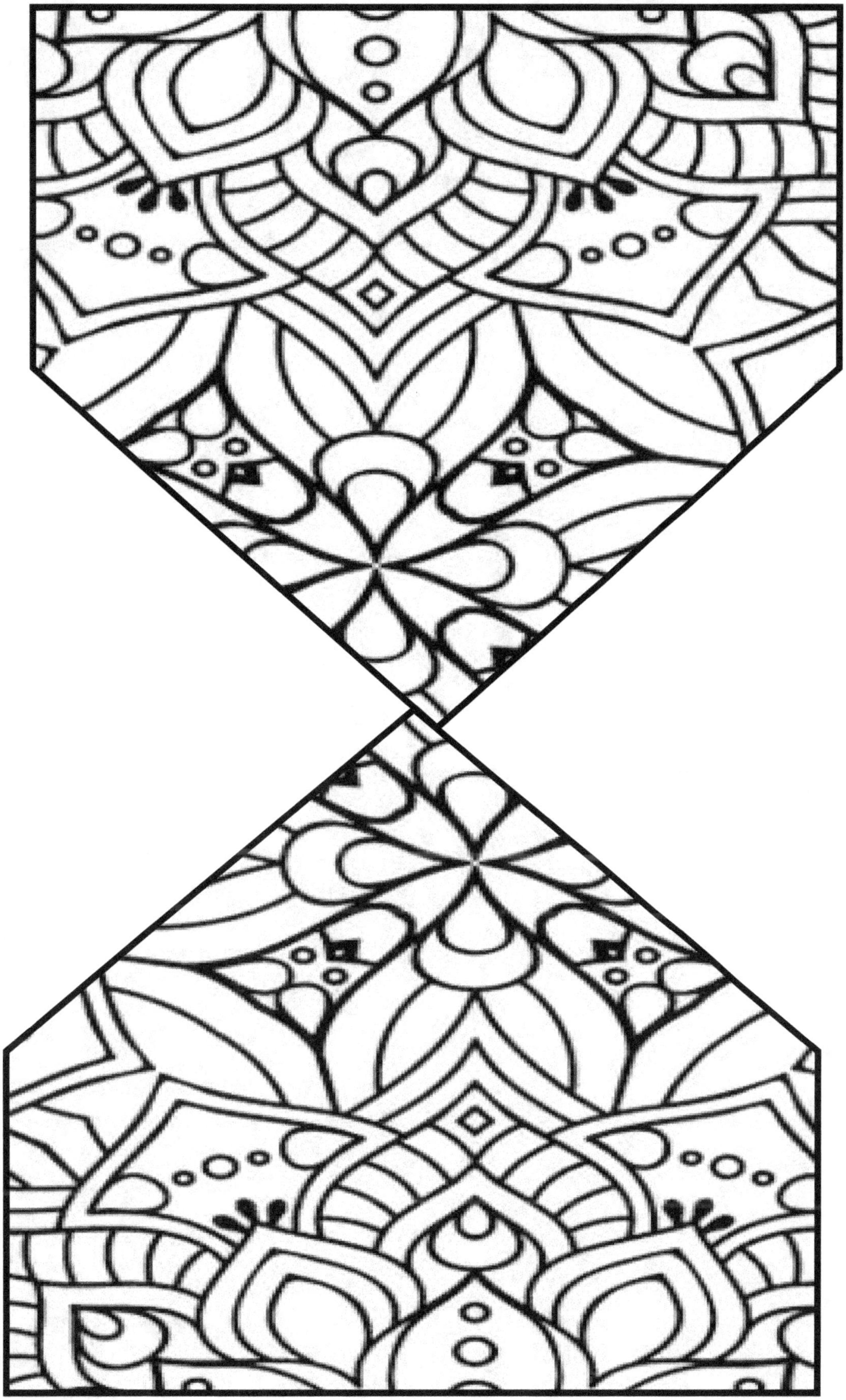

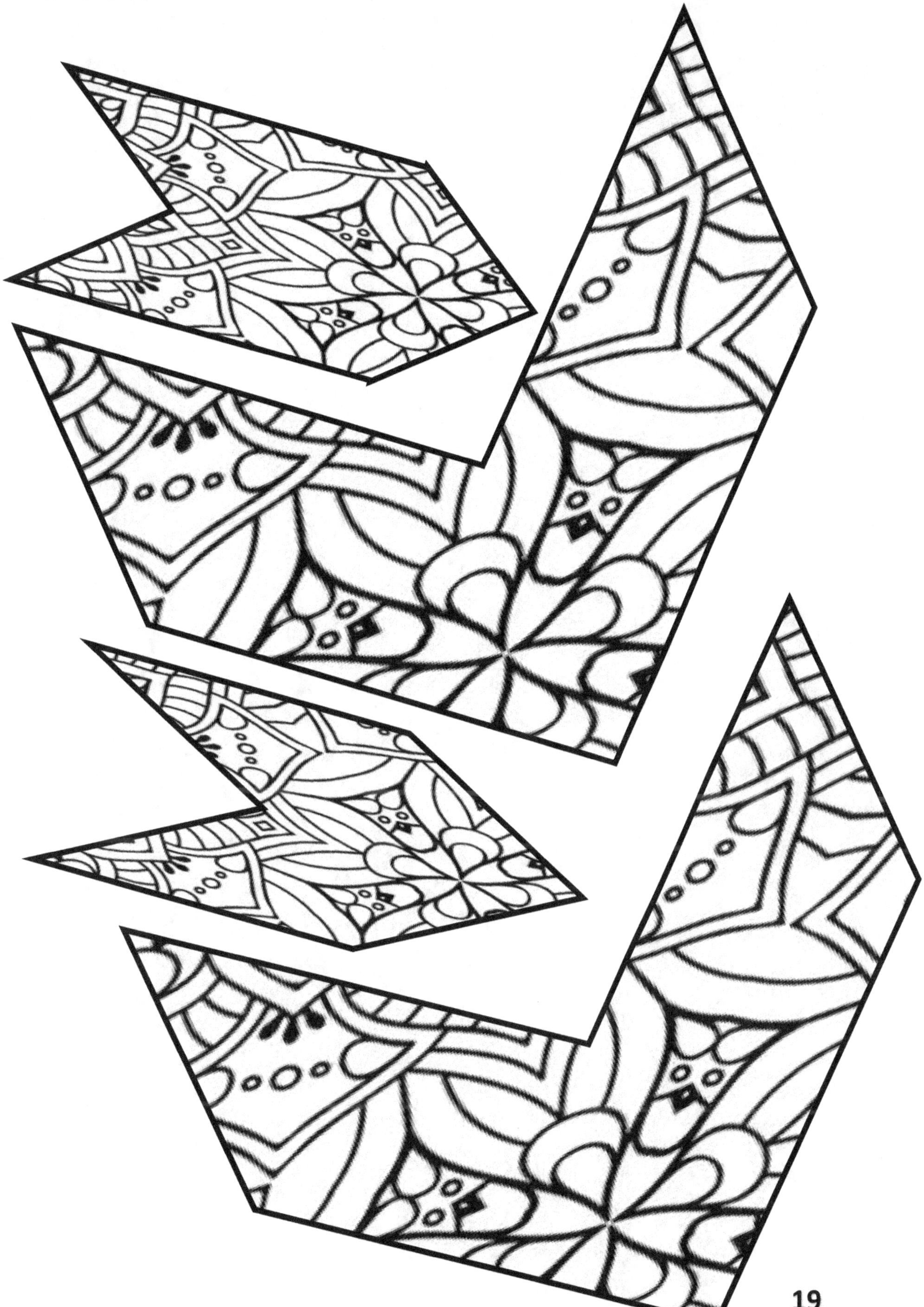

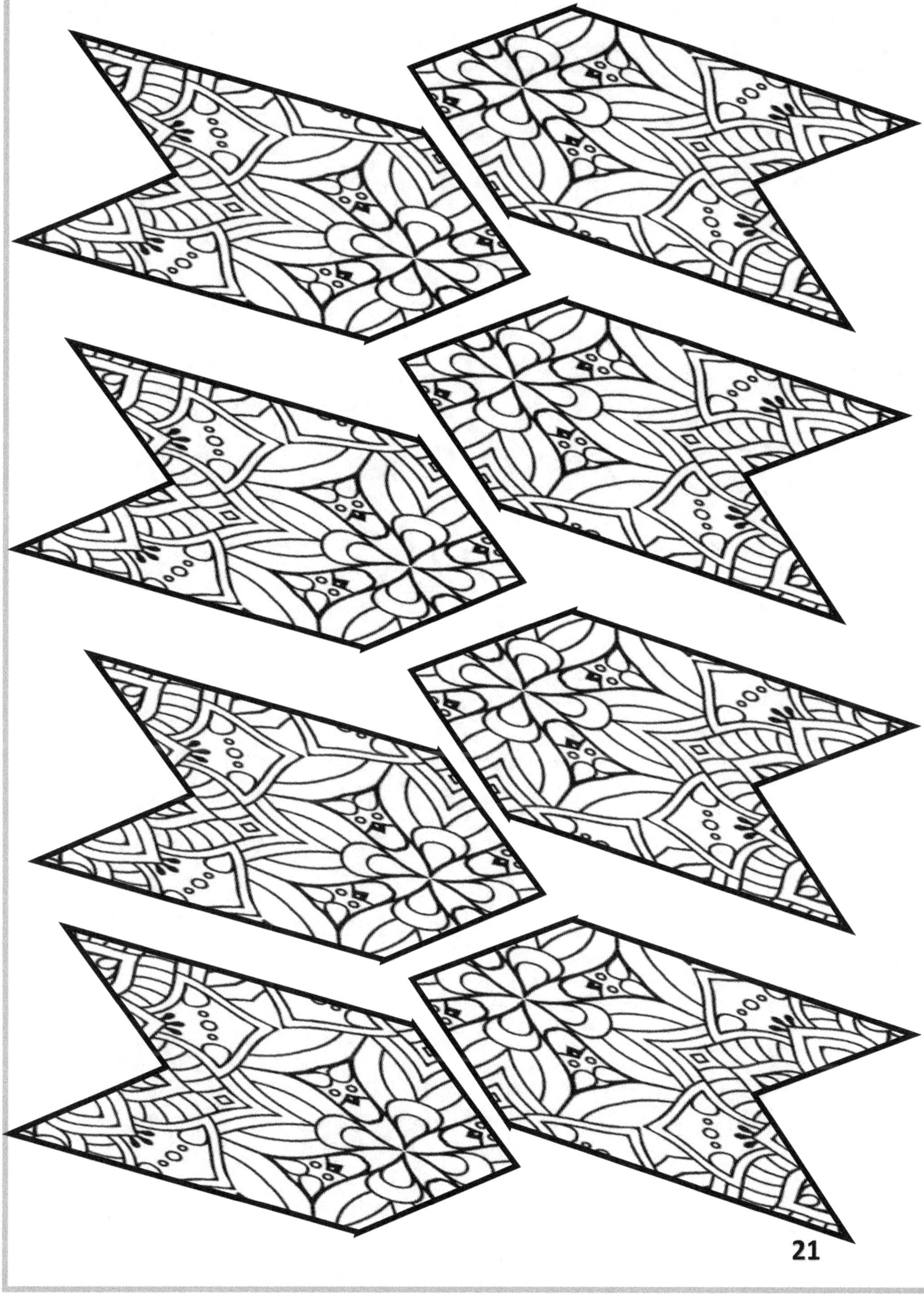

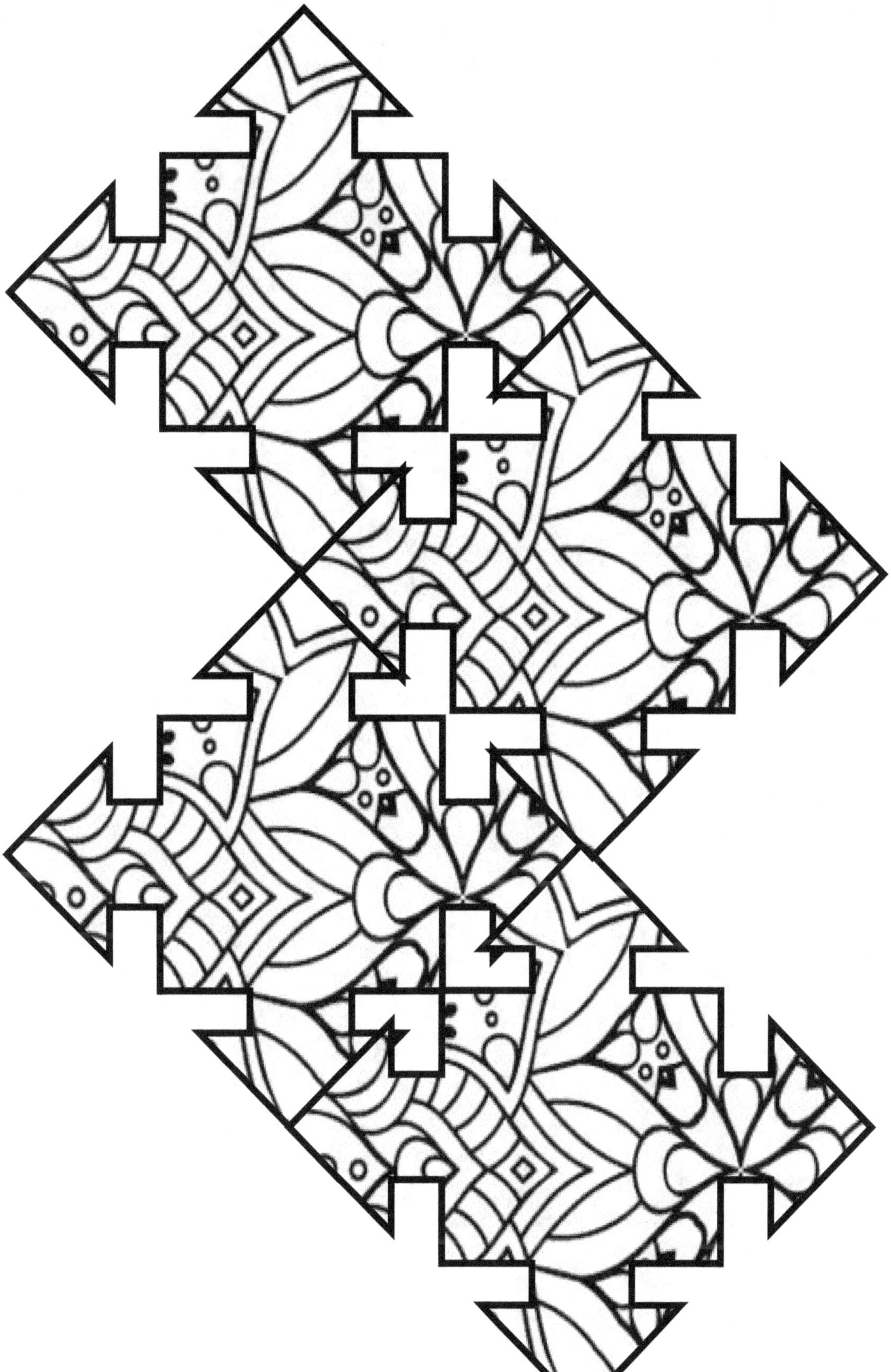

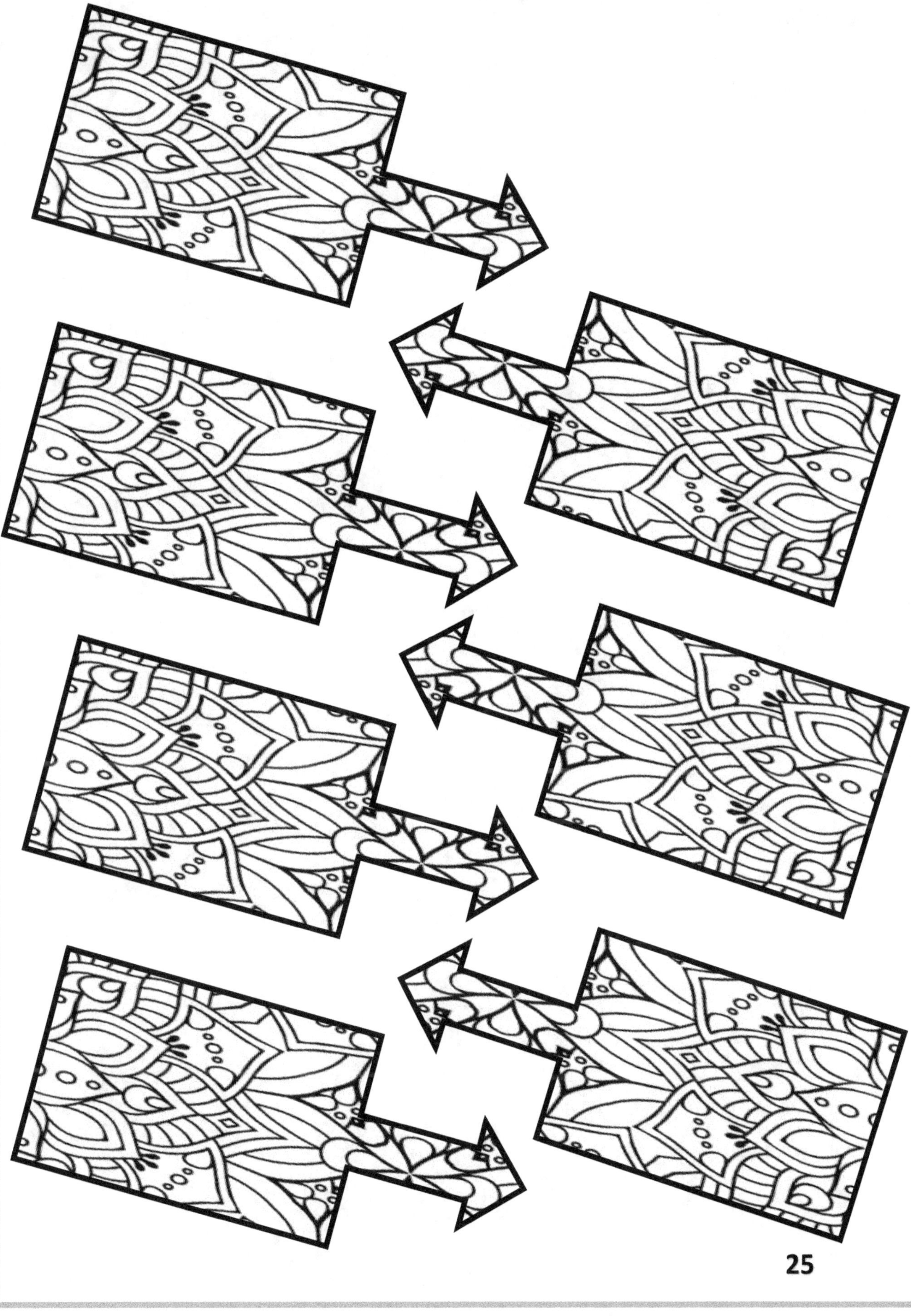

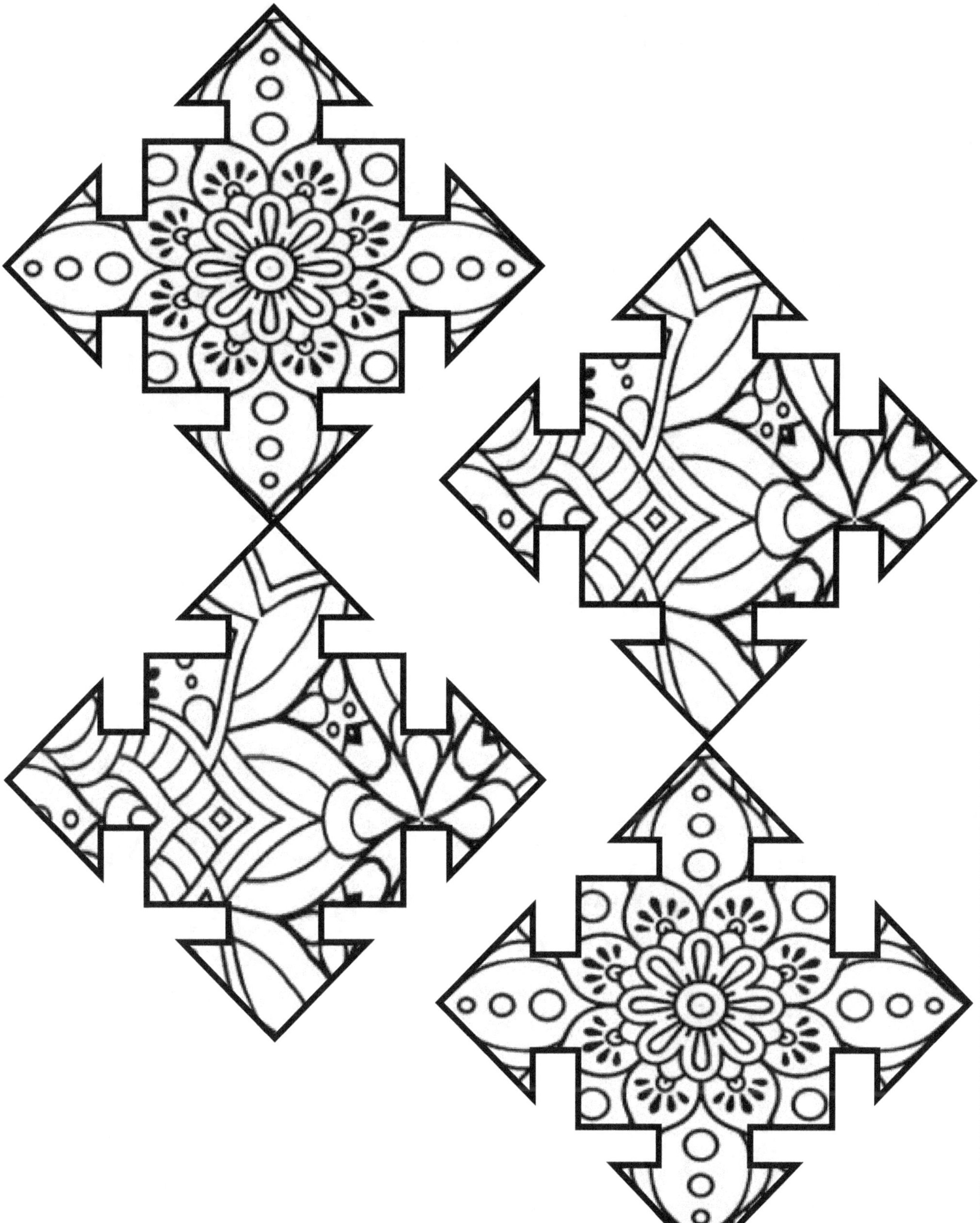

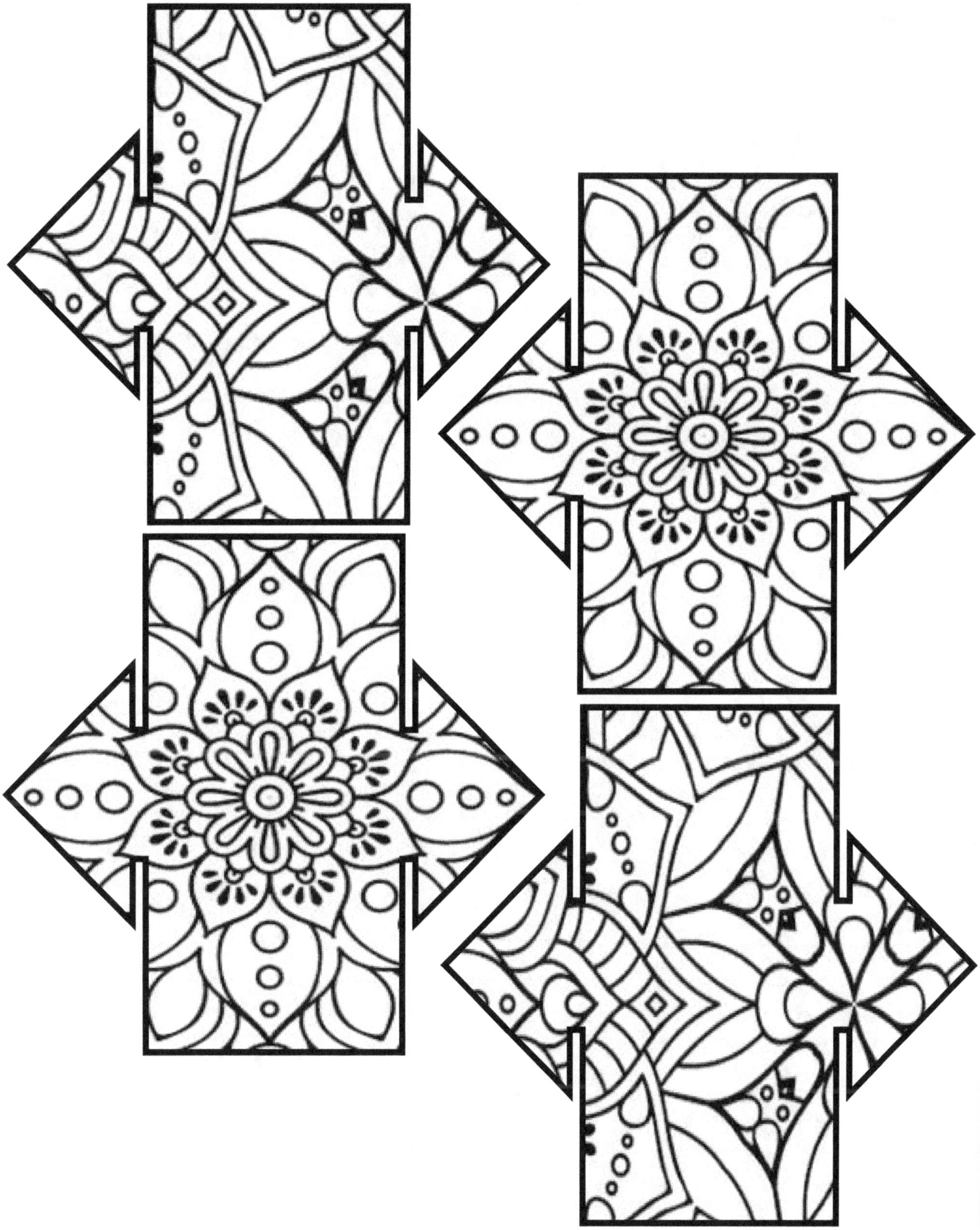

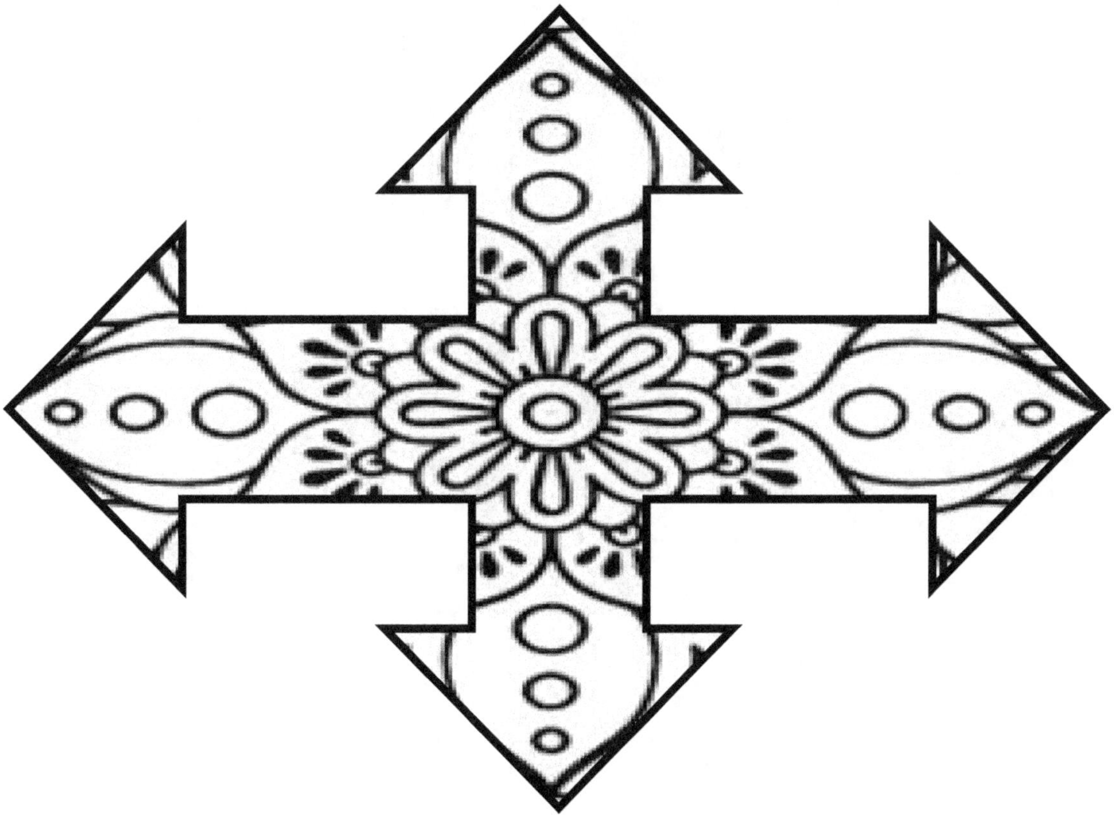

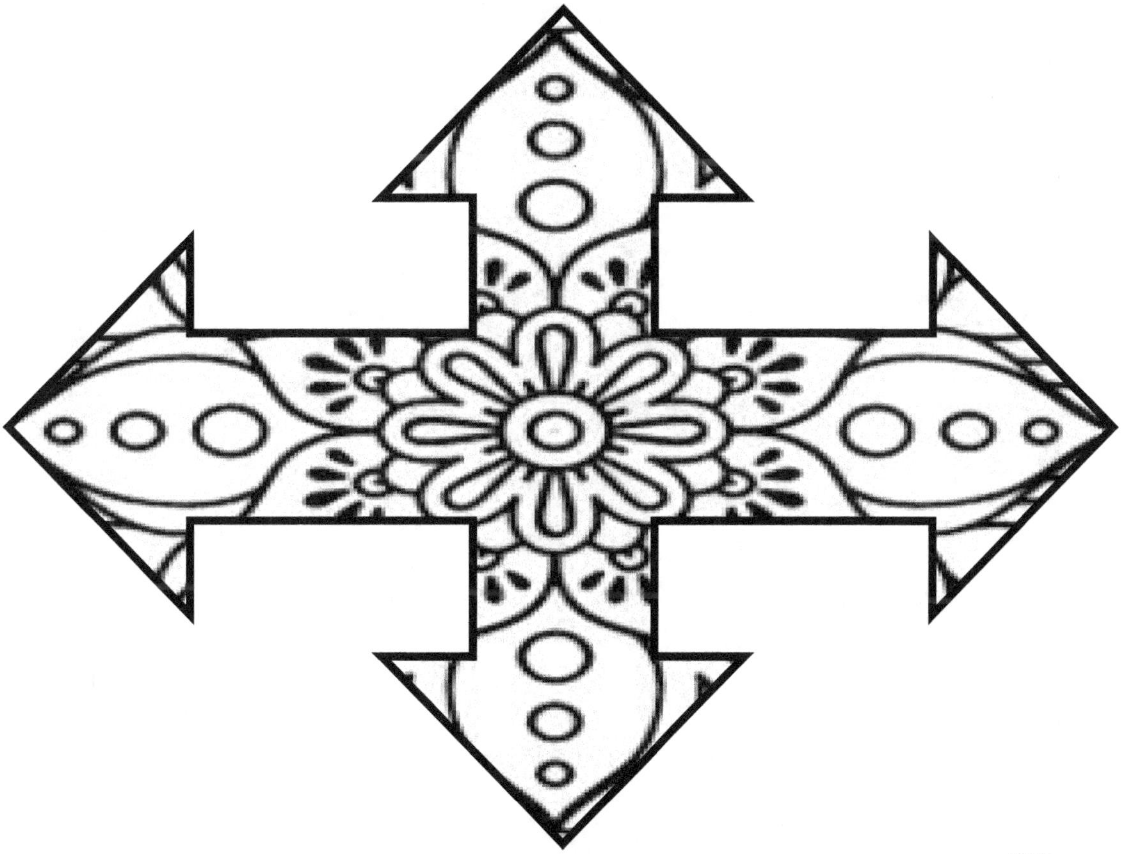

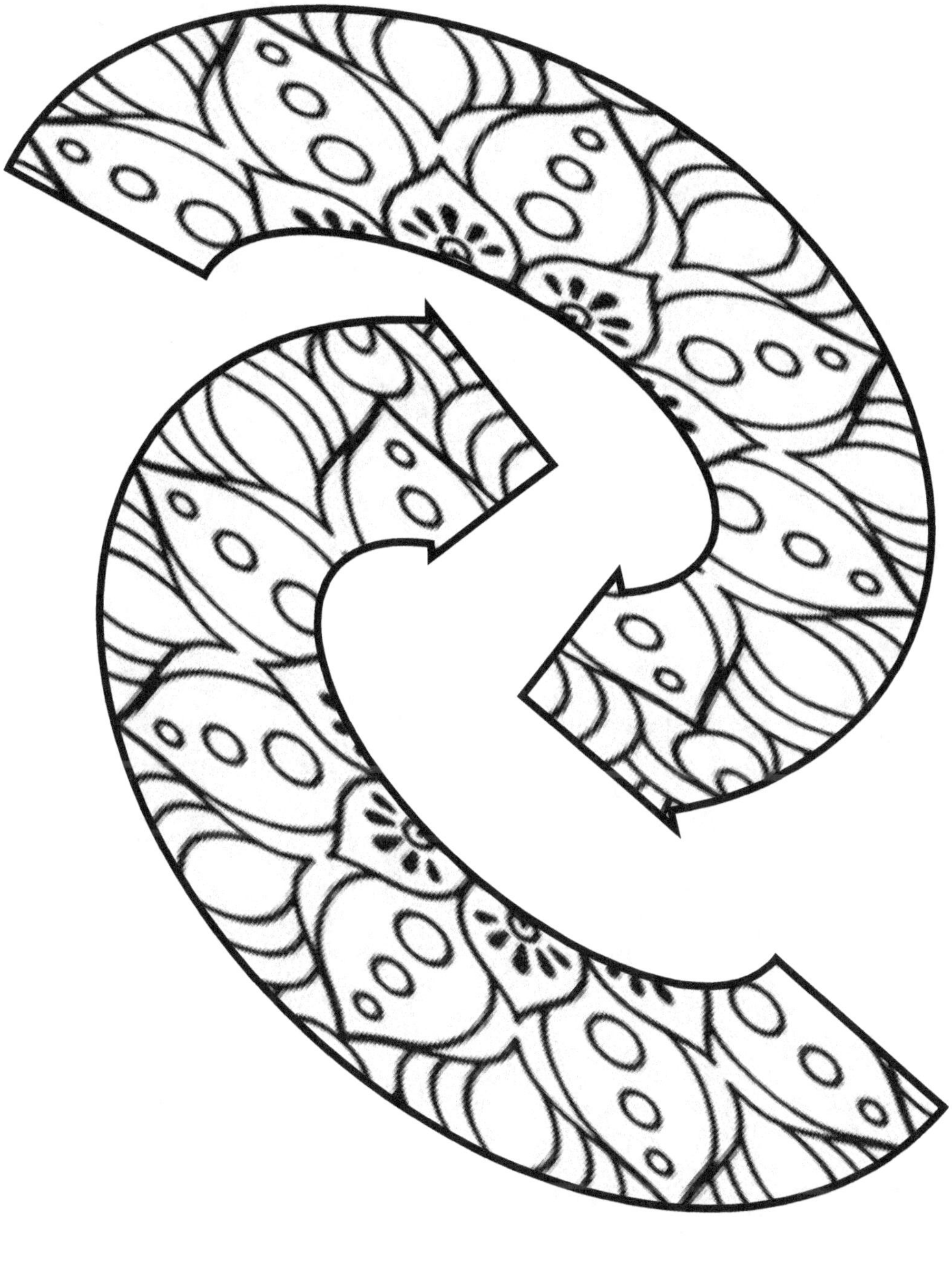

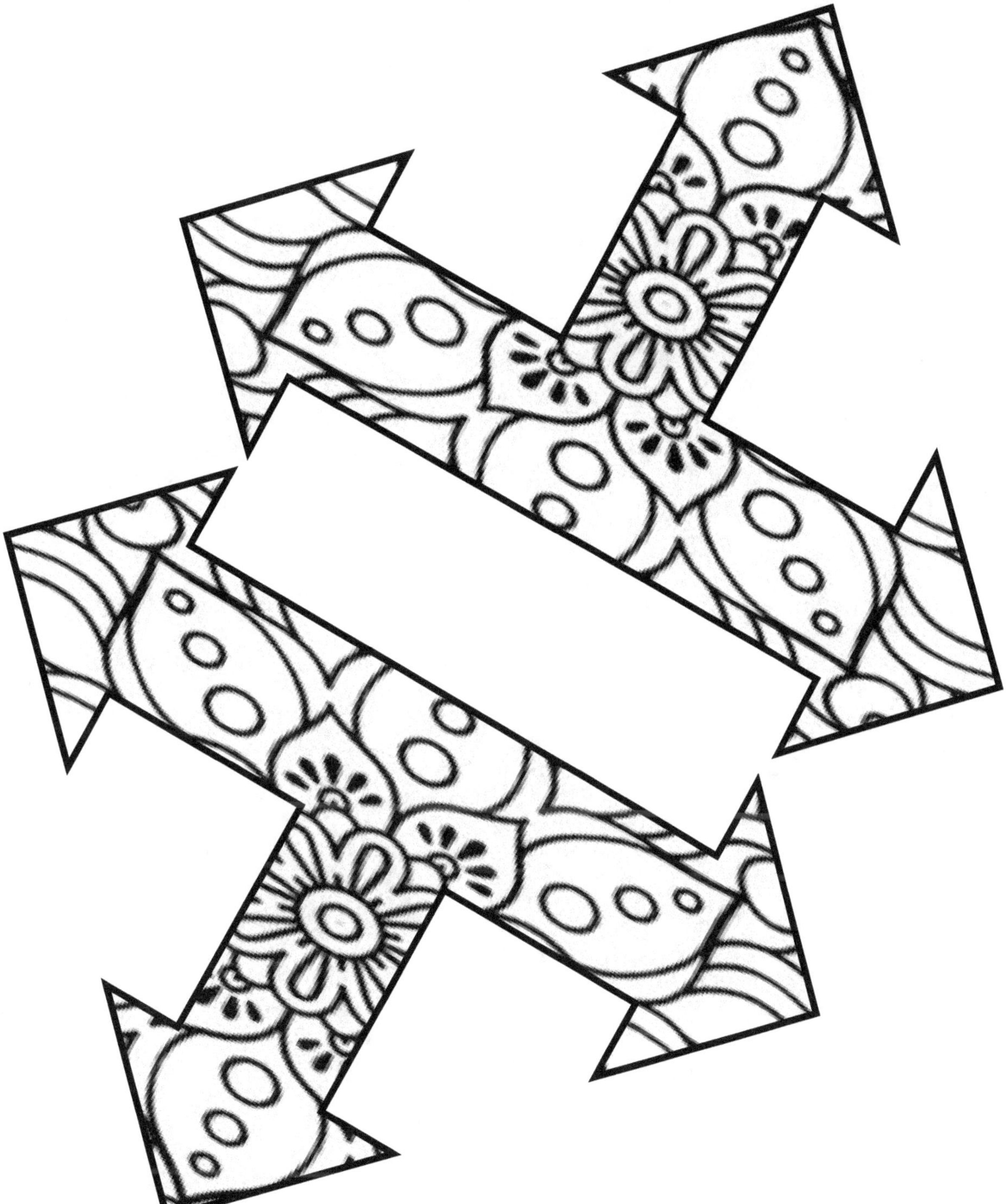

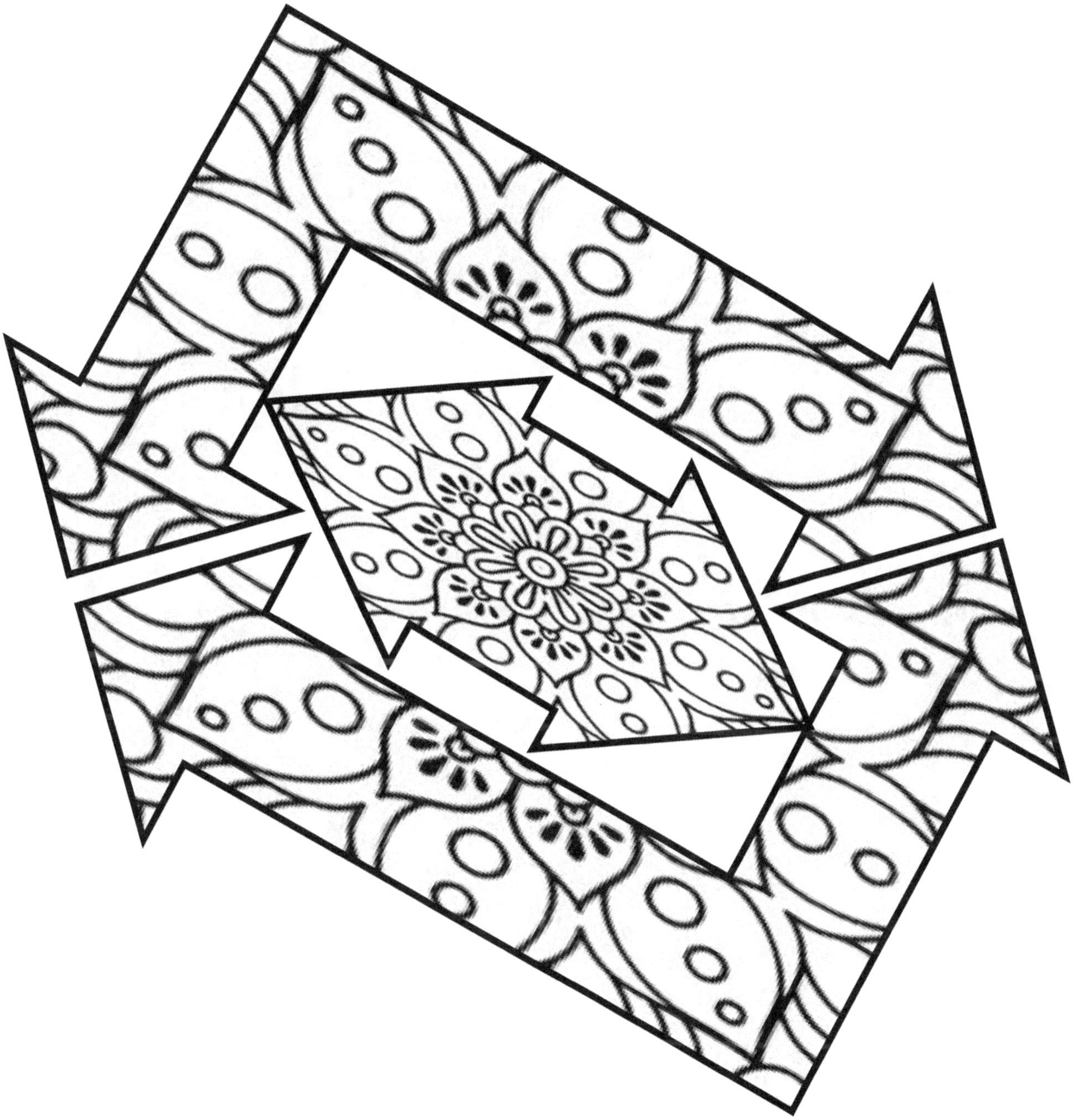

www.ingramcontent.com/pod-product-compliance
Lightning Source LLC
Chambersburg PA
CBHW080628220526
45467CB00011B/3411
9798706646783